THE
ART
AND
WORDS
OF MY
EXPERIENCE

JEAN MARIE PATTY

PROMINENT
BOOKS

5830 E 2nd St, Ste 7000 #9983
Casper, WY 82609
USA

Contents

A Gift from God

God gave me a gift that
I wasn't sure I deserved.
He was ever so kind and
Perhaps a bit reserved.

He stole my heart away
It caught me by surprise.
I found it hard to believe
But he said he liked my eyes.

God decided it was time
For me to be content.
It took a while to see but
I knew just what it meant.

I had finally done my time
But never saw my worth.
The years were quite unkind
But He led me to rebirth.

Jean Marie Patty

A Place of Beauty

There is a place that
I would like to go.
It's not on this earth
It's much greater though.

A place filled with laughter
A place full of fun.
It's some place awesome
But I've only just begun.

It's a place filled with love
And beauty beyond belief.
It will take your breath away
And there will be no grief.

Heaven is the only place
I really want to see.
Nothing else compares
And that you can believe.

Jean Marie Patty

Angel on my Shoulder

It was three in the afternoon
And all was quiet.
But something would happen
To cause such a riot.

She knew not his name
But he carried a gun.
There was nowhere to go
And nowhere to run.

A calm came over her
And all was silent.
But the intentions were ugly
And also quite violent.

She begged and she pleaded
And the angels were there.
She asked him to leave
And he told her "Beware"!

Jean Marie Patty

Beautiful Man

There was a young girl
Filled with dreams and zeal.
But time left a scar
That no one could heal.

Then one fine day
She met a beautiful man.
He was dressed in a robe
And he took a great stand.

He whispered in her ear
Of a love so divine.
Then before her very eyes
Turned water into wine.

Jean Marie Patty

***** *Tantalizing Trio* *****

Christmas

Christmas is a lovely time
For everyone to rejoice.
The angels are singing and
We hear the sweet voice.

The angels sing for Jesus
They sing for everyone.
Let's all sing our praises
To the most important One.

The season is so bright
And filled with so much cheer.
It makes us thankful as we
Look to a peaceful new year.

It's nice to wrap presents
And think of all the fun.
But don't forget about Jesus
For He is the greatest One!

Jean Marie Patty

Count Your Blessings

When you are feeling down
Think of another's fate.
The ability to walk
Is something to appreciate.

The gift of vision
Is a beautiful sight.
Consider life in the dark
That's an awful fright.

Always count your blessings
Through every single day.
The Lord is merciful
With Him we should stay.

Jean Marie Patty

Emotional One

Do you share the same opinion?
I really need to know.
But if you choose to ignore me,
I cannot let it go.

I've tried and tried to forget
But the scars they run too deep.
Every time I try to communicate,
It only makes me weep.

I wish they could understand
What it's like to be me.
But no one seems to want to know,
And it just won't set me free.

Jean Marie Patty

Everlasting Love

How do we find it
True and everlasting love?
Look around and you will see
It only comes from above.

Life is most uncertain
So find time to pray.
It may sound rather simple
But it's really the only way.

Look to each beautiful day
And always give God praise.
There's a bright shining sun
With the most breathtaking rays.

Jean Marie Patty

***** Lady Lantern *****

Fluffy Feather

Feather is my kitten
She just ran up her tree.
She is so very fluffy
She's as pretty as can be.

Feather is so very sweet
I love her to the end.
She is so very kind and
She'll always be my friend.

Feather is so very soft
And funny as can be.
I love all my kitties
And that you can believe.

Jean Marie Patty

Forever I Will Pray

I need you in my life
I want you more each day.
I cry out your name Lord
Forever I will pray.

Lord, your kindness heals
You make my heart grow warm.
Forever I will walk with you
Through any kind of storm.

I cry when I pray
Because I feel your love.
Lord, you are so beautiful
You are sweeter than a dove.

I cannot live without you
Now that I've seen your light.
You have truly blessed me
I am smiling with delight.

Jean Marie Patty

Forgive

Little girl lost
Where have you gone?
We miss you so much
But we have to move on.

We try to forget
All that we hate.
But He is the Savior
We rush to the gate.

If the gate is closed
We've lost our soul.
So we must forgive
And then become whole.

Jean Marie Patty

Give Him the Glory

Lord, I love you so much
I want to let it show.
Lord, I love you dearly
More than you'll ever know.

You make my heart happy
Your wisdom means so much.
I love your beautiful creations
And your precious loving touch.

I sing your praises daily
I give you all the glory.
For you give me the desire
To tell everyone your story.

Jean Marie Patty

***** Awesome Angels *****

God is Everywhere

God, I know you're out there
I see your beauty everywhere.
I see it in the trees
I hear it in the breeze.

Your love is everywhere
I see it in the flowers.
Your love is so complete
It fills up all the hours.

I used to feel alone
But now I am fulfilled.
You blessed my life completely
For that I am so thrilled.

Jean Marie Patty

God is Love

God is the answer
God is all you need.
His love is everlasting
And no one can exceed.

God can hear you crying
He can make you feel alive.
No one can do better
We need him to survive.

God gives us love
That no one can compare.
You see it in the ocean
You see it in the air.

It's written in the stars
We can see it in the sky.
His love is so powerful
It will make you feel so high.

Jean Marie Patty

God Loves the Animals

When I see an animal
I know that God is real.
So many beautiful creations
So much love to feel.

I know God loves the animals
For He created them all.
They are so amazing
From the great to the small.

No other being could
Be so innocent.
Their love is pure
They are magnificent.

Jean Marie Patty

He Cares

The Lord picked me up
When I was down.
He taught me to smile
Instead of to frown.

He lifted my spirits
Beyond all compare.
He helped me to breathe
When there was no air.

The Lord can help you
In your time of need.
He listens to everyone
He cares deeply indeed.

When He is our role model
We cannot go wrong.
He can hear our prayers
We praise Him in song.

Jean Marie Patty

***** Ornate Cross *****

He Knows Us All

The writing is a gift
That only God can provide.
He is our salvation
From Him we should not hide.

We must give God the glory
For He knows us all.
We can never give up
He will not let us fall.

The moment we give up
The heart will surely die.
It's a lonely place to be
But in God we can rely.

We must speak God's name
In order to survive.
He will drown our sorrows
He will make us feel alive.

Jean Marie Patty

Heaven

I hope this letter finds you well
And everything is alright.
I think about you everyday
And almost every night.

I really miss you and I
Wish that you were here.
I can't believe you're really gone
Sometimes I feel you're near.

I hope we meet again someday
And I know that you are well.
I'm sure there is a Heaven
And I know that it is swell.

Some people think it's silly
To dream of life above.
But I believe in Heaven
It's filled with beauty and love.

Jean Marie Patty

His Everlasting Way

I awake with the sun
I awake brand new.
I turn to the Lord
And I know He is true.

He whispers softly in my ear
The sounds are oh so sweet.
He gives me strength and guidance
And a place where I retreat.

Take time to listen
To all He has to say.
Take time to observe
His everlasting way.

Jean Marie Patty

His Gracious Love

Lord, you know my heart
You know how much I love you.
God's love is forever
His ways are always true.

I cannot live without
God's pure and gracious love.
We need it to help us grow
It only comes from above.

God's light is ever present
His love will light the way.
His forgiveness is a blessing
We should cherish Him everyday.

Jean Marie Patty

***** Agape Angel *****

In His Presence

Time is very precious
Time is of the essence.
It was ever so lovely
To be in His presence.

I could feel His love
Surrounding my soul.
His love is omnipresent
It made me feel whole.

I could feel the spirit
Rushing through my mind.
They sounded like angels
Their voices so kind.

We were all smiling and
Listening to the word.
The sounds of Heaven and
The sweetness was heard.

Jean Marie Patty

Keep the Faith

The Lord spoke to me and
This is what He said.
Never lose your faith
Without it you are dead.

Sometimes the road is long
But listen to your heart.
He will never forget you
You will not fall apart.

The Lord gives us strength
He is so very sweet.
He listens when we speak
His words we must repeat.

He heals the loneliness
And He is always kind.
Never forget His love
It fills your heart and mind.

Jean Marie Patty

Kind and Loving Ruth

Ruth is kind and as
Sweet as she can be.
She makes me feel loved
And lives her life free.

Ruth loves the Lord
And obeys His word.
She would never stray
His word is all she heard.

Ruth has inspired me
In many ways.
She appreciates her life
And lives for all the days.

Jean Marie Patty

Life's Uncertain Path

If you choose a certain path
You may find different things.
Some are looking for love
Some look for diamond rings.

There is so much more to find
On life's unsteady road.
Some are paved with sadness
And some are paved with gold.

It's best to never give up
For there are many dreams.
Some will find them all
Others keep searching it seems.

It seems we all search for
The path in life to take.
Search yourself and you will find
That God will never forsake.

Jean Marie Patty

***** Love Hurts *****

Love is True

Our love is so true
I really have to say.
You mean so much to me
I will never go away.

I love you today as
I did the day before.
My love will surely grow
And that you can be sure.

So do not be afraid
Of losing this sweet love.
It is my special gift that
Comes from up above.

For my love is a gift
Which God has given me.
He put the love in us.
It truly sets us free.

Jean Marie Patty

Miss Martha

Martha listens to all
I have to say.
She never judges
She is just that way.

She welcomes friends
Into her lovely home.
She took care of the elderly
And made them feel less alone.

Martha is kind to
Everyone she knows.
She lives for Jesus
Her love for Him shows.

Jean Marie Patty

Missing Isaiah

I miss you Isaiah
I miss you so much.
I had to learn how
To live without your touch.

I wish I could hold you
And watch you play.
But I'll just have to wait
For that sweet precious day.

I know you are in Heaven
And happy with our Lord.
But I am so lonely
And I often feel bored.

I cannot wait to see you
I hope it won't be long.
I will think of you often
And remember you in song.

Jean Marie Patty

My Dog Bailey

You are my buddy
I love you so.
You make me happy
And that's all I know.

You're kind and sweet
And you never judge.
You are so special
You don't hold a grudge.

My Bailey loves me
No matter what.
He is always friendly
I love him so much.

Jean Marie Patty

***** Beautiful Bird *****

My Friend Karen

My dear friend Karen
She is so very kind.
She is always thoughtful
She knows the ties that bind.

My sweet friend Karen
Fills my heart with love.
She is a child of God
She was sent from above.

My true friend Karen
Inspires me with her wisdom.
She talks of love for Jesus
She will reign in his kingdom.

Jean Marie Patty

My Kitten Willow

Willow is the sweetest kitten
And soft as she can be.
She doesn't play that much
But she will run up a tree.

Willow is soft spoken but
She also likes to squeal.
We love her cute meow
It is really quite surreal.

When Willow was a baby
She played all the time.
But now she is older
I think she is sublime.

We love her more than life
And that you can be sure.
She's absolutely beautiful and
Our love for her is pure.

Jean Marie Patty

My Love For You

I will always love you
As a matter of fact.
I will always care
No matter how you act.

You are so funny
And thoughtful as can be.
You always put me first
And you do it gladly.

No one else cares
The way that you do,
Except for Jesus
And that is true.

I do love you
Every single day.
I still love you
In each and every way.

Jean Marie Patty

My Love is Forever

Do you know I love you
Do you know I care?
My love is forever
Our love is what we share.

Do you understand the depths
Of this love I have for you?
It is truly amazing
My love is always true.

I care beyond belief
I know you are aware.
I care with all my heart
Our love it seems so rare.

Jean Marie Patty

***** Spot & Dot *****

Precious Lord

Hear me oh Lord
I know your glory.
He is forever love
His is the greatest story.

I will walk with you
And follow your commands.
I will love you always
I know you hold my hands.

You are precious Lord
You make everything right.
I will trust you always
I will live in your light.

Jean Marie Patty

Rising Sun

There is a sad story
Of shame and of woe,
But the ending is happy
And we'll never know.

We'll never know why
The child was so sad.
She cried and she cried
And thought she was bad.

The years passed on
Still sure of her doubt.
She doubted she could
Love herself all about.

Then faced with adversity,
Much to her surprise,
Something would change:
The sun would soon rise.

Jean Marie Patty

Sharing Secrets

I remember that night
Filled with secrets and fright.
He whispered in my ear
Things I did not want to hear.

But heard them I did
And all was out loud,
The sorrow and pain
Of secrets not proud.

Why did he choose me?
I will never know.
But my life changed,
I was filled with woe.

Jean Marie Patty

So Tragic

There he was just yelling
Accusations in my ear.
He was ranting and raving
Things I did not want to hear.

How could this be true?
I really did feel hurt.
I never could have imagined
That I would feel like dirt.

For the ones you think you know
Are not always what they seem.
It is so very tragic
That he could be so mean.

Jean Marie Patty

***** Pretty Peacock *****

Sweet Frances

Fran is the sweetest
Person that I know.
Just look at her face
You can see her glow.

Fran gave me hope
When there was despair.
She listened to me
And gave loving care.

I love my Frannie
With all my heart.
She gave my life meaning
Right from the start.

Thanks to sweet Fran
I can live in the light.
She is truly an angel
She shines so bright.

Jean Marie Patty

Sweet Sara

There was a kitten named Sara
Who stole my heart away.
Her disposition was ever so sweet
And she loved to run and play.

She filled my life with laughter
But then she had to leave.
My heart did weep in sorrow
And I found it hard to believe.

It seemed there might not be a God
Which left me feeling sad.
But after a bit of time had passed
The pain didn't seem so bad.

Jean Marie Patty

The Beginning

She whispers a song
So sad and blue.
She wants to be heard
And wants to be true.

No one is listening
And she wonders why.
Life is uncertain
We all have to die.

Death isn't the end
Of a painful journey.
It's the beginning of something
Wondrous and yearning.

It is nothing to fear and
It's nothing to hate.
It is a beautiful place
Filled with untimely grace.

Jean Marie Patty

The Christmas Gift

I woke up this morning
And couldn't believe my eyes.
It was a wonderful day
What a great surprise.

I never really noticed
But suddenly there it was.
The answer I'd been wanting
Was answered just because.

He didn't leave me presents
But I didn't even care.
He gave me a greater gift
He promised He'd always be there.

For if you make the choice
To believe in His word,
He will never forsake and
You will always be heard.

Jean Marie Patty

The Image They Uphold

They think that I am wrong
Because I take a stand.
They tell me not to speak
And wouldn't that be grand.

They often do manipulate
It really is a shame.
I would like to be indifferent
But things just never change.

They must remain on top
In order to maintain
The image they uphold,
But I really must abstain.

Spare me the propaganda
It really does grow old.
I can't stand to hear it again
I was never really sold.

Jean Marie Patty

The Lonely Clown

There was a young girl
Who was dressed like a clown.
She was never smiling
Only wearing a frown.

When someone asked her
"Why do you frown?"
She suffered in silence
And only looked down.

She had no explanation
For the sadness and fear.
She kept her mouth shut
And she tried not to hear.

Only endless despair
Was left in the air.
She never knew why
Life seemed so unfair.

Jean Marie Patty

The Sword

In my moment of darkness
I have seen much despair.
Life can be so lonely and
Happiness can seem so rare.

But lift your spirits high
And look up to the Lord.
For He can answer all your prayers
And He will give you the sword.

For the sword you need
Is that of wisdom and love.
Live to fulfill all your dreams
And always look up above.

Jean Marie Patty

Time Stood Still

Love is everywhere
Love is oh so dear.
Take nothing for granted
And have nothing to fear.

Only time can tell
But promises are kept.
The years passed away
But still she wept.

She was longing for something
That only He could fill.
The void was apparent
And time stood still.

Jean Marie Patty

***** The Lonely Clown *****

Tragedy of a Nation

Twin towers are torn apart
On this most horrible day.
We must stand united and
We definitely need to pray.

Let's pray for the children
Who have lost their mothers.
Let's pray for the sisters
Who have lost their brothers.

For families have been divided
And it makes us very sad.
We must rebuild our nation
But we're also really mad!

Jean Marie Patty

We Are One

Love is true
So are you.
Dark is night
Sky is blue.

Love is fine
You are mine.
We are one
Together in time.

Mine is yours
Yours is mine.
Together we love
In life sublime.

Jean Marie Patty

Words from God

I know this to be true
The words all come from God.
When you listen to this poem
It may not seem so odd.

God gives us wisdom
He also gives us love.
It's written in His book
It's sweeter than a dove.

I know God hears our prayers
I've seen it time and again.
There's never been a better day
To make anew and begin.

We begin to hear the birds
And we see God in the trees.
His beauty is in everything
His love will set you free.

Jean Marie Patty

You Are Everything

I want you to be my lover
And also to be my friend.
I want you to be my everything
Until the very end.

Life would be so lonely
If you were not in it.
I never want to imagine
Life without your spirit.

For you are everything to me
You are so caring and kind.
To think of life without you
Would simply blow my mind.

Jean Marie Patty

***** Ornate Confusion *****

If anyone has any

comments about this book,

you may send them to:

Jean Marie Patty
P.O. Box 4574
Anniston, AL 36204

www.ingramcontent.com/pod-product-compliance
Lightning Source LLC
Chambersburg PA
CBHW031236120626
46545CB00003B/1136